NEW YORK

EXPLORE THE UNITED STATES

Julie Murray

Big Buddy BOOKS
Explore the United States

VISIT US AT
www.abdopublishing.com

Published by ABDO Publishing Company, PO Box 398166, Minneapolis, MN 55439.

Printed in the United States of America, North Mankato, Minnesota.
042012
092012

 PRINTED ON RECYCLED PAPER

Coordinating Series Editor: Rochelle Baltzer
Editor: Sarah Tieck
Contributing Editors: Megan M. Gunderson, BreAnn Rumsch, Marcia Zappa
Graphic Design: Adam Craven
Cover Photograph: *Shutterstock*: Donald R. Swartz.
Interior Photographs/Illustrations: *AP Photo*: AP Photo (pp. 23, 25), File (p. 13), Frank Franklin II (p. 21); *Getty Images*: Yves Marcoux (p. 26); *Glow Images*: Donald Nausbaum (p. 27), Marvin Newman (p. 21); *iStockphoto*: ©iStockphoto.com/aivolie (p. 29), ©iStockphoto.com/genekrebs (p. 19), ©iStockphoto.com/nancykennedy (p. 5), ©iStockphoto.com/makalu (p. 17), ©iStockphoto.com/DenisTangneyJr (p. 9), ©iStockphoto.com/veni (p. 9); Shutterstock: Melinda Fawver (p. 30), iofoto (p. 13), Nancy Kennedy (p. 27), Philip Lange (p. 30), Brian Lasenby (p. 30), Caitlin Mirra (p. 11), Stuart Monk (p. 26), Sari Oneal (p. 30), SeanPavonePhoto (p. 19), SVLuma (p. 27), Andy Z. (p. 11).

All population figures taken from the 2010 US census.

Library of Congress Cataloging-in-Publication Data

Murray, Julie, 1969-
  New York / Julie Murray.
    p. cm. -- (Explore the United States)
  ISBN 978-1-61783-370-0
  1. New York (State)--Juvenile literature. I. Title.
  F119.3.M87 2013
  974.7'1--dc23
                        2012010560

Contents

One Nation 4

New York Up Close 6

Important Cities 8

New York in History 12

Timeline 14

Across the Land 16

Earning a Living 18

Sports Page 20

Hometown Heroes 22

Tour Book 26

A Great State 28

Fast Facts 30

Important Words 31

Web Sites 31

Index 32

One Nation

The United States is a **diverse** country. It has farmland, cities, coasts, and mountains. Its people come from many different backgrounds. And, its history covers more than 200 years.

Today the country includes 50 states. New York is one of these states. Let's learn more about New York and its story!

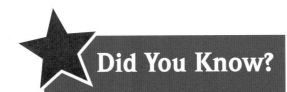

Did You Know?

New York became a state on July 26, 1788. It was the eleventh state to join the nation.

The Hudson River flows through New York.

5

NEW YORK UP CLOSE

The United States has four main **regions**. New York is in the Northeast.

New York has five states on its borders. Vermont, Massachusetts, and Connecticut are east. New Jersey and Pennsylvania are south. The country of Canada is northwest. The Atlantic Ocean is southeast.

New York has a total area of 53,095 square miles (137,515 sq km). About 19 million people live there. That makes it the third most-populated state!

REGIONS OF THE UNITED STATES

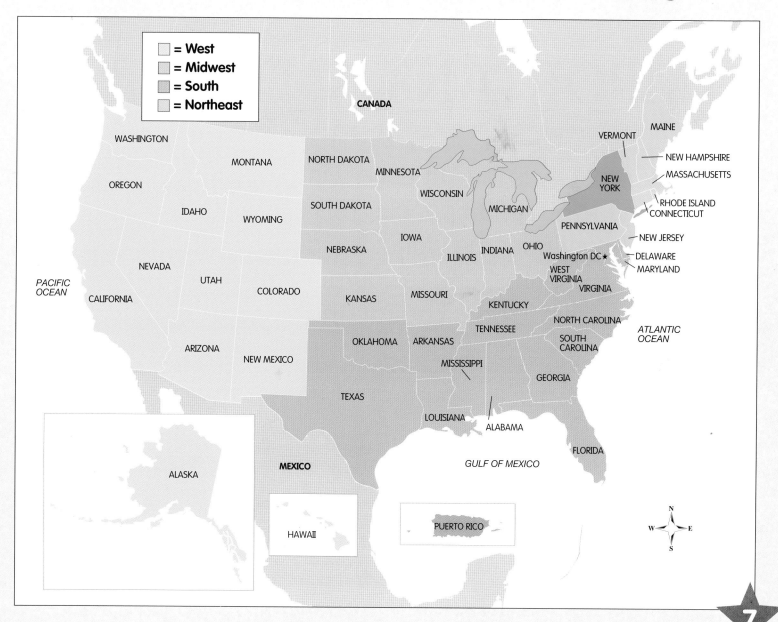

= West
= Midwest
= South
= Northeast

CANADA

WASHINGTON

MONTANA

NORTH DAKOTA

MINNESOTA

VERMONT

MAINE

OREGON

IDAHO

WYOMING

SOUTH DAKOTA

WISCONSIN

MICHIGAN

NEW
YORK

NEW HAMPSHIRE

MASSACHUSETTS

RHODE ISLAND

CONNECTICUT

PENNSYLVANIA

NEW JERSEY

IOWA

NEVADA

UTAH

COLORADO

NEBRASKA

ILLINOIS

INDIANA

OHIO

Washington DC ★

DELAWARE

MARYLAND

PACIFIC
OCEAN

CALIFORNIA

KANSAS

MISSOURI

WEST
VIRGINIA

VIRGINIA

KENTUCKY

ARIZONA

NEW MEXICO

OKLAHOMA

ARKANSAS

TENNESSEE

NORTH CAROLINA

SOUTH
CAROLINA

ATLANTIC
OCEAN

MISSISSIPPI

GEORGIA

TEXAS

LOUISIANA

ALABAMA

FLORIDA

ALASKA

MEXICO

GULF OF MEXICO

HAWAII

PUERTO RICO

N
W   E
S

7

IMPORTANT CITIES

New York City is the largest city in the United States! It is home to 8,175,133 people. This city is a leading business center for the world. It is also home to famous theaters, museums, and restaurants.

Albany is New York's **capital**. This historic city on the Hudson River became the capital in 1797. It is known for its **architecture**.

Did You Know?

New York City is made up of five areas called boroughs (BUHR-ohs). They are Manhattan, Brooklyn, Queens, the Bronx, and Staten Island.

New York

Rochester
Buffalo
Albany ★
New York City

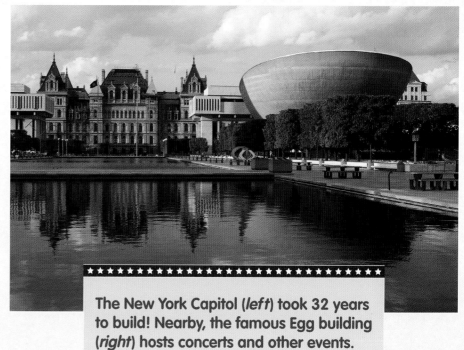

The New York Capitol (*left*) took 32 years to build! Nearby, the famous Egg building (*right*) hosts concerts and other events.

The United Nations is based in New York City. This worldwide group works for peace.

Buffalo is New York's second-largest city, with 261,310 people. It lies at the start of the Niagara River. Many people stay in this city when they visit nearby Niagara Falls.

Rochester is the third-largest city in the state. It is home to 210,565 people. This city is known for its history. It became a village in 1817. The Erie Canal was built through it. This important waterway connects Lake Erie to the Hudson River.

Buffalo is home to many businesses.

The Erie Canal opened in 1825.
Companies use it to ship goods.
This helped Rochester grow.

11

NEW YORK IN HISTORY

New York's history includes Native Americans and **immigrants**. Native Americans lived on the land for thousands of years. The first European explorers arrived in the 1500s. Settlers came in the 1600s. In 1788, New York became a state.

The growth of business drew many immigrants to New York. Between 1892 and 1924, about 12 million people arrived from around the world.

An immigration center called Ellis Island opened in 1892. Immigrants passed through it when they came to the United States.

Today, Ellis Island is a museum.

13

Timeline

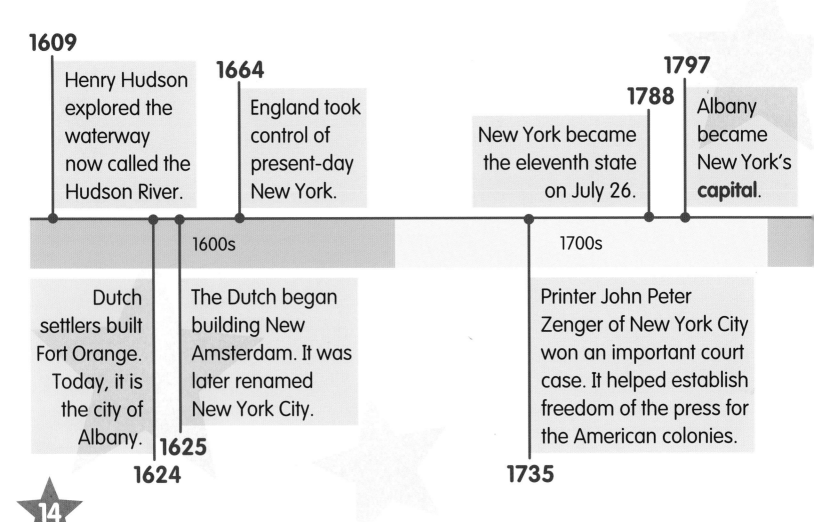

1609

Henry Hudson explored the waterway now called the Hudson River.

1664

England took control of present-day New York.

1797

Albany became New York's **capital**.

1788

New York became the eleventh state on July 26.

1600s

1700s

Dutch settlers built Fort Orange. Today, it is the city of Albany.

The Dutch began building New Amsterdam. It was later renamed New York City.

Printer John Peter Zenger of New York City won an important court case. It helped establish freedom of the press for the American colonies.

1625

1624

1735

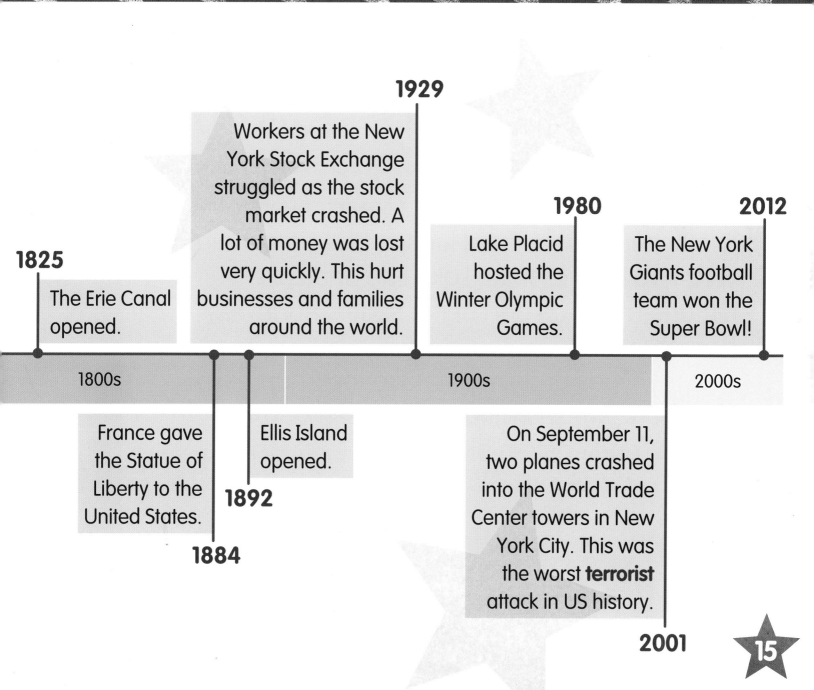

1929

Workers at the New York Stock Exchange struggled as the stock market crashed. A lot of money was lost very quickly. This hurt businesses and families around the world.

1980

Lake Placid hosted the Winter Olympic Games.

2012

The New York Giants football team won the Super Bowl!

1825

The Erie Canal opened.

1800s

1900s

2000s

France gave the Statue of Liberty to the United States.

Ellis Island opened.

1892

On September 11, two planes crashed into the World Trade Center towers in New York City. This was the worst **terrorist** attack in US history.

1884

2001

15

ACROSS THE LAND

New York has mountains, forests, rivers, lakes, and coasts. The Hudson River is a major waterway in the state. Lake Erie and Lake Ontario make up part of the state's northwest border.

Many types of animals make their homes in New York. These include beavers, red foxes, rabbits, and eastern bluebirds.

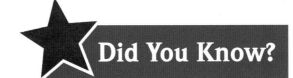

Did You Know?

In July, the average New York temperature is 69°F (21°C). In January, it is 21°F (-6°C).

People visit New York's Adirondack Mountains to hike, ski, and swim.

Earning a Living

New York is known around the world for its strong businesses. Many people work for banks, restaurants, and hotels. Others work for the government.

Shipping, manufacturing, and **media** are also important in New York. Many magazines, books, newspapers, and news and television shows are made there.

Northern New York is known for dairy farming.

The New York Stock Exchange is located on Wall Street in Manhattan. It is important to businesses around the world.

19

SPORTS PAGE

New York is home to many famous sports teams. The New York Giants, New York Jets, and Buffalo Bills play football. The New York Knicks play basketball. And, the New York Mets and New York Yankees play baseball.

New York hosts important sporting events, too. The US Open is held in New York City each year. Also, the Belmont Stakes horse race takes place every year near New York City.

Did You Know?

New York has hockey teams, too! The New York Rangers are one of the oldest teams in the National Hockey League.

★★★★★★★★★★★★★★★★★★★★★★★★

The Belmont Stakes is one of three horse races that make up the Triple Crown.

★★★★★★★★★★★★★★★★★★★★★★★★

The US Open is one of four major tennis events around the world.

21

HOMETOWN HEROES

Many famous people are from New York. Theodore Roosevelt was born in New York City in 1858. He was the twenty-sixth US president. He served from 1901 to 1909.

Roosevelt was vice president in 1901 until President William McKinley was killed. When Roosevelt took over, he became the youngest US president. He was just 42 years old! As president, Roosevelt set aside land for national parks.

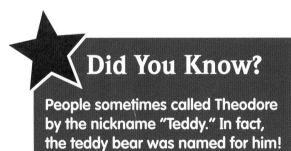

Did You Know?

People sometimes called Theodore by the nickname "Teddy." In fact, the teddy bear was named for him!

23

Franklin D. Roosevelt was born in Hyde Park in 1882. He was a distant cousin of Theodore Roosevelt. He became the thirty-second US president in 1933. Roosevelt served until his death in 1945. He was the only president to be elected four times!

Roosevelt was famous for helping the United States through the **Great Depression**. He started programs to help people get jobs, food, and homes. And, he led the country during **World War II**.

Did You Know?

Past US presidents Martin Van Buren and Millard Fillmore were also from New York.

At age 39, Roosevelt lost the use of his legs from a disease called polio. He worked very hard to stand and walk after this. Few people knew of Roosevelt's disability.

Tour Book

Do you want to go to New York? If you visit the state, here are some places to go and things to do!

 ## Watch

Take in a Broadway show. Broadway is a famous New York City avenue. Many important theaters are on and around it. They feature some of the world's best live shows!

 ## Explore

See the Adirondack Mountains in northern New York. Mount Marcy is the state's highest point. It is 5,344 feet (1,629 m) tall.

 ## ⭐ Discover

Visit New York City's Statue of Liberty. You can walk up inside of it! Check out other famous places in the city, such as Central Park and Times Square.

⭐ Learn

Visit the United States Military Academy at West Point. This is the country's oldest military college. The oldest US military museum is there, too!

⭐ Cheer

Catch a New York Yankees baseball game! They play at Yankee Stadium in New York City. Many people consider them one of the best Major League Baseball teams!

A GREAT STATE

The story of New York is important to the United States. The people and places that make up this state offer something special to the country. Together with all the states, New York helps make the United States great.

Niagara Falls is one of New York's natural wonders.

Fast Facts

Date of Statehood:
July 26, 1788

Population (rank):
19,378,102
(3rd most-populated state)

Total Area (rank):
53,095 square miles
(28th largest state)

Motto:
"Excelsior"
(Ever Upward)

Nickname:
Empire State

State Capital:
Albany

Flag:

Flower: Rose

Postal Abbreviation:
NY

Tree: Sugar Maple

Bird: Eastern Bluebird

Important Words

architecture a style of building.

capital a city where government leaders meet.

diverse made up of things that are different from each other.

Great Depression the period from 1929 to 1942 of worldwide economic trouble. There was little buying and selling, and many people could not find work.

immigrant someone who has left his or her home and settled in a new country.

media ways of sharing information, especially with large groups of people. Radio, television, newspapers, and magazines are examples of media.

region a large part of a country that is different from other parts.

terrorist a person who uses violence to scare or control people or governments.

World War II a war fought in Europe, Asia, and Africa from 1939 to 1945.

Web Sites

To learn more about New York, visit ABDO Publishing Company online. Web sites about New York are featured on our Book Links page. These links are routinely monitored and updated to provide the most current information available.

www.abdopublishing.com

Index

Adirondack Mountains **17, 26**
Albany **8, 14, 30**
animals **16, 30**
Atlantic Ocean **6**
Belmont Stakes **20, 21**
Buffalo **10, 11, 20**
businesses **8, 11, 12, 15, 18, 19**
Canada **6**
Central Park **27**
Ellis Island **13, 15**
England **14**
Erie, Lake **10, 16**
Erie Canal **10, 11, 15**
Fillmore, Millard **24**
France **15**
Hudson, Henry **14**
Hudson River **5, 8, 10, 14, 16**
Hyde Park **24**
Lake Placid **15**
Marcy, Mount **26**

Native Americans **12**
Netherlands **14**
New York City **8, 9, 14, 15, 19, 20, 22, 26, 27**
Niagara Falls **10, 29**
Niagara River **10**
Northeast (region) **6**
Ontario, Lake **16**
population **6, 8, 10, 30**
Rochester **10, 11**
Roosevelt, Franklin D. **24, 25**
Roosevelt, Theodore **22, 23, 24**
size **6, 30**
statehood **4, 12, 14, 30**
Statue of Liberty **15, 27**
Times Square **27**
US Open **20, 21**
Van Buren, Martin **24**
weather **16**
West Point **27**
Zenger, John Peter **14**